To My Family, for sharing in this journey.
And to our living planet, for providing the beauty along the way.

—SMB

To Louise and Eloise — my energy and inspiration.

—JL

Sleeping Bear Press®
2395 South Huron Parkway, Suite 200
Ann Arbor, MI 48104
www.sleepingbearpress.com

Printed and bound in the United States.

10 9 8 7 6 5 4 3 (case)
10 9 8 7 6 5 4 (paper back)

Library of Congress Cataloging-in-Publication Data

Bestor, Sheri Mabry, author.
Good trick, walking stick! / written by Sheri Mabry Bestor ;
illustrated by Jonny Lambert.
pages cm
Audience: Ages 6-8.
Summary: "Walking sticks are among the world's most fascinating insects.
And one many children can find right in their backyards! With a simple
story, perfect for read-alouds, this scientific look at a walking stick's
life-cycle will captivate budding entomologists"— Provided by the
publisher.
ISBN 978-1-58536-943-0 Hard Cover
ISBN 978-1-58536-981-2 Paper Back
1. Stick insects—Juvenile literature. I. Lambert, Jonny, illustrator. II. Title.
QL509.5.B47 2016
595.7'29—dc23   2015027642

Good Trick, Walking Stick!

By Sheri Mabry Bestor and Illustrated by Jonny Lambert

Drop,

plop.

Drop.

Tiny eggs fall to the ground,
like a slow rain on an autumn day.

Leaves float on the breeze and hide the eggs. The air turns crisp. Snowflakes drift. The woods are covered in a blanket of white.

Underground, buried deep, the eggs are safe.

Brrr! You might wonder how tiny walking stick eggs survive through the winter in the snow. The eggs look and smell like seeds to ants. When the ants find the eggs hidden under the leaves, they carry the eggs into their colony as food. The ants eat the tops off the eggs, just like they would eat the tops off of seeds. When they are finished, the ants drag the uneaten parts to their garbage dump area, still underground. Even though the tops have been eaten away, the eggs are not harmed. The eggs incubate, hidden in the ant nest, away from predators, until they are ready to hatch.

When spring comes, the sun melts the snow.

Drip,

        drip,

drip.

        It warms the earth.

An egg moves.

Wiggle wiggle wiggle, POP!

Out crawls an insect. It looks like a stick. It can walk.
It is a walking stick!

Do you think you would recognize a just-hatched
walking stick? They look like tiny adult walking
sticks! Walk gently through the woods so the
plants and animals aren't disturbed.

The baby walking stick is hungry.
She begins her search for food.

She finds a leaf that is low to the
ground. She eats.

Munch!

And eats.

Munch!

A baby walking stick is called a nymph and is very small when it hatches. Although they begin tiny, when they grow up, some walking stick species are among the longest known insects in the world!

And eats!

Munch. Munch.

As the baby walking stick eats, she grows. As she grows, her outer shell, or casing, becomes tight. The baby walking stick wiggles and stretches. She sheds her casing and grows a new one.

Shedding a casing, or exoskeleton, and growing a new one is called molting. When one exoskeleton is shed, the body growing inside hardens and forms a new exoskeleton.

The walking stick blends into the forest.

Good trick, walking stick!

One of a walking stick's best tricks is its ability to be camouflaged—it looks like its surroundings. That way, predators can't see it. If you are in an area where walking sticks might be living, you can challenge yourself to be a super detective. See if you can spot a stick insect!

But here comes a bird with keen eyes. Swoop!
It grabs the walking stick.

The stick insect squirts a bad-smelling juice. Ick!
The bird spits the walking stick out.

When a bird lands on a twig the twig quivers. Stick insects quiver in the same way. This slight movement by the stick insect is called "quaking."

Uh-oh!

The young stick insect has lost a leg! That is all right.
She will grow a new one when she grows a new casing.

Good trick, walking stick!

The walking stick will molt six times
before she is fully grown. One form
of defense for a young walking stick
is the ability to lose an appendage,
or leg. This is called autotomy.

The stick insect climbs, looking for food.

Up...   up...   up...

she goes.

The tree has many leaves. The stick insect will not go hungry. The tree is filled with other stick insects. She will not be alone.

Using two claws and a
suction cup on each foot,
the adult stick insect is a
good climber.

In the light of the day, she sits perfectly still on a twig. She has turned colors to match the bark.

Good trick, walking stick!

Some species of walking stick are able to change color with light or temperature. On a sunny day, the stick insect can turn lighter. That helps it stay hidden in the sunlight and stay cooler. At night, the insect darkens in color. It can then stay warmer and hidden in the dark. Being able to change color is one reason it is so tricky to spot a stick insect.

Along comes a hungry squirrel. Uh-oh!

The stick insect sways in the breeze with the branches. The squirrel comes near. Its tail brushes the stick insect. Too close!

Quick as a sneeze, the stick insect pulls in her legs and drops to the forest floor, just like a stick falling off a larger branch. The squirrel scurries away.

The stick insect is safe.

Good trick, walking stick!

The walking stick doesn't move. All day,
she stays still. She can't run fast. She can't fly.
She can only hide, camouflaged like a stick.

Some species of walking stick do have wings and can fly. They keep their wings folded and hidden. When a predator approaches, they flash their wings open. The bright, colorful wings startle the predator and help buy time for an escape!

The sunlight fades. Darkness comes. It is safer now, so the walking stick climbs back up into the tree. She joins the other walking sticks. She has changed color to match the night.

Good trick, walking stick!

Because most of their predators aren't out searching for food at night, walking sticks are safer when it's dark. But some bats eat walking sticks, and any movement can be picked up with bats' echolocation—no matter how dark it is! So watch out, walking sticks!

In the dark, birds are no longer looking for food. Squirrels rest. Only night animals move.

Munch munch.

Crunch. Munch.

The walking sticks move around too, eating leaves.

They eat... and eat. And eat.

Summer begins to fade. Colors pop out on the leaves.
Female stick insects spritz their perfume into the cooling air.

Male walking sticks smell the perfume. They choose mates.

This stick insect does not find a mate.

Alone, she sits on a twig until, from high in the tree,
one at a time, her eggs fall to the forest floor.

Drop,

plop.

Drop.

It is like a slow rain on an autumn day.

Female stick insects can produce eggs even without a mate. This is called parthenogenesis. If the eggs are not fertilized, they will hatch into female walking sticks.

Frost lulls the woods towards winter sleep.
The air turns crisp and snowflakes drift to the
forest floor.

But the eggs are safe.

Under the snow, inside the seed-like shells,
the walking stick's daughters are growing.

Until one day the snow melts.

Drip,
        drip,
drip.

And spring blooms...

Wiggle wiggle wiggle, POP!

Out walk more stick insects!

Good trick, walking sticks!

Even though it seems like it would be fun to have a stick insect as a pet, it is important to let stick insects live in their natural surroundings. Enjoy nature with your ears and eyes. Listen and watch!